# BLINK.

Sawyer Benjamin

Illustrations and cover art by

Mallory Ballou

Copyright © 2020 by Sawyer Benjamin

All rights reserved. No part of this book may be reproduced or used in any manner without written permission of the copyright owner except in the context of reviews.

Illustrations and cover art by Mallory Ballou

Paperback: 9781735643489

E-Book: 9781735643458

First edition

To any and all of you who may see yourselves within these pages

- both literally and figuratively.

Thank you for allowing me to be a part of your stories. It was an honor to include you in mine.

**Contents**

06. A Note to Readers

08. Dead·name

11. You are Five Years Old, a Pink Denim Straight Jacket of Rocks and Fuss and Comic Books

13. Baby Blue

14. Jack, Drew, and Finn

15. In Which We Were Both at Chuck E. Cheese and You Were Told to Thank the "Big Boy" that Helped You Defeat Galaga

16. Depilatory

17. Cabin Fever

20. The Queer Community's Ode to the Oxford Comma

22. Period Sex

24. The Locusts and the Cottonwoods

26. She

28. heavens

29. He

31. Hermit

32. Baby Blue II

33. Baby Blue III

34. Her Recycled Sock (Remains Unaware of What They are Building Today)

35. Pulse

41. Yellow : Tangerine : Bittersweet

42. Cirque du Comparaison

47. First Body

48. Password Security Questions for Transphobes on Twitter

50. Anemoia

59. 04/09/2019

61. Euphemism for Pissing

65. Inferno

66. Asexual Musings

75. Baby Blue IV

76. Blink

79. Acknowledgements

80. About the Author and Illustrator

*"This is a call to arms*

*for the poets that are inside of us."*

- Paradise Fears,

Prelude

**A Note to Readers**

The poems in this collection were inspired by the real-life experiences of myself and other LGBTQIA+ individuals, and thus contain content that may be troubling to some readers. These topics include, but are not limited to:

mental health,

reclamation of queer and trans slurs,

pregnancy,

menstruation,

religion,

violence,

sex,

sexual assault,

internalized transphobia and homophobia,

gender dysphoria,

suicide,

death,

and various forms of anti-LGBTQIA+ discrimination.

The author encourages you to be mindful of these and other possible triggers, and remember to practice self-care as necessary before, during, and after reading.

**Dead·name**
\ ˈded-nam \

*noun*


1. His mother swore she was the next Dave Chapelle.

Said naming a Christmas Eve born

after a season decked in blistering heat

and communal holy water stoups

was almost as funny as the coincidence of he,

East Palomar Street's newest edition

of a so-called female,

sharing his *first* first name

with the so-called *feminine* hygiene products

shelf-stacked, first in line to tell him

his vagina was a dirty word.


2. One hundred and four days of each year

spent palming pennies from coincidence

for just a lick of freedom and

Lucas Limon con Chile from the ice cream truck.

He found that timing

deadbolt latch to speaker blare

held more value than any math class

and when he was lucky enough

to add asphalt blisters to his soles

he was no longer girl or boy,

or grounded or beat down,

but lightning bug disappearing

into the San Diego skyline.


**3.** He once misheard a friend say

to put olive oil on a sunburn.

He didn't know how he had made it

so many trips around the sun

only experiencing how it felt

 to cook from the inside out.

 But, he imagined that somewhere out there

  was a little girl, also tearing open

  birthday cards that weren't addressed to her,

  lugging around G.I. Joe's and baseball cards

  that should have been pom-poms and Polly Pockets,

  and wondering about him,

  and if his wishes, too, caught fire

  each time his skin cells multiplied.

**See:** *heatstroke.*

**See:** *ankles latched in rip current confusion.*

**See:** *every cocked head. Every broken record when, and why, and how.*

**See:** *forecasts of fresh sunflowers and sun kissed braids*

    *when he has always been more earthworm*

    *and earth between his knuckles.*

**You are Five Years Old, a Pink Denim Straight Jacket of Rocks and Fuss and Comic Books**

    Flirt with girls.

                          Bring them rocks and wilted flowers

        and let them win every chase.


    Raise your voice.

           Spit verses at the top of your lungs

                    and don't mind the fuss you make.


    Take a hike through the woods.

        Go deep without a compass

and completely lose your way.


    Play with bugs.

           Collect two of each kind

        and build an ark out of your pockets.


    Sock your cousins in the eye.

                        Wrestle with your uncle.

        Fight back at your father.


                Don't bother

        with force-feeding your time

on fad diets and dance.

Pants were made to get dirty.

                Dig your nails in the mud

  and rip holes in your knees.

        Read superhero comic books

and teach yourself to fly

  from the tallest tree in the yard.

             Run fast and fall hard.

    Scrape up your elbows.

Maybe get a stitch or two.

                    Do all the things that you can't do

  'cause grown-ups tell you no.

            They'll say those things are meant for boys.

                        *... Guess they told you so.*

I tried to write to you today

but the words felt too foreign.

My mother tongue has never known

the things a father should say.

- **Baby Blue**

**Jack, Drew, and Finn**

when the princesses begin to sing to him is when he finds it safe to go to sleep. finally, he hears their tender lull; a precious comfort far and feather-down, and as he musters up his bed of straw he spends his sweet time noising along with them. his own a mouse between the cracks, still sometimes catches wind and then sometimes, there are swallows or knuckles thimbled, brashed. his homeland was built far from castle but still tempts poison apples in its psalms; and he knows he will not Chance a sleeping bag under his wing for the play date tomorrow. not because mother told him no. or because he was not invited - six different times, in fact, after the initial envelope scrawl. but, because the other boys had never spoken of their princesses before. so, he would run and play with bugs and cars and Jacks and match just how they Drew their swords until his lungs fell flat and the sun was down and the River in his veins ran dry, and then he would return. coven up into his room, long after his homeland was all Tuckered in, and he would sit on edge with feet of Finns and wait until the princesses began to sing again.

**In Which We Were Both at Chuck E. Cheese, and You Were Told to Thank the "Big Boy" that Helped You Defeat Galaga**

You were maybe four, or five, no older than six,
and I was a snowstorm jacket in July, pizza
face and greasy fingers that knew jack shit
about you or me, but did know that your tears
were not worth enough tickets for a toy soldier
and that you had to go left to aim right, and that
the second button from the top required a slightly
larger hand to push in all the way, and that
the best trick to save long hair from snagging on
the machinery was to hide it in a baseball cap,
and that I had never been called a big boy before,
and, maybe, *I* should have thanked *you* instead.

**Depilatory**

When the first man I ever loved,
but never wanted as a lover, ask
ed me to help him get ready
for his date, I did not expect for
him to invite that tall, dark, and
hands-on bottle into our cramped
apartment bathroom, nor for the
image of him, a bare-bottomed
starfish, bent over the same
sink I rinsed my filth down twice
a day to be what comes to mind
now, when asked about queer
love, and how it comes
boundless and unconditional.
But, what else could queer love
be besides abandoned souls in one
small home, finally free to laugh
until they cry and cry until they
laugh and turn crimson, but, only
because they chose to all while
allowing one another to shed
  their most guarded parts?

She sparked

fire from

her fingertips

lit her

ablaze with

her kiss

and stacked

her bones

inside the

fireplace

to keep

them warm

through winter

with eyes

so evergreen

and fists

full of

snowfall she

closed their

curtains with

her teeth

to keep

away the

outside world

swore they

would never

need fresh

air then

built her

lungs into

a crawl

space stole

her breath

in isolation

'til forests

couldn't hear

her scream

but when

the smoke

built up

too thick

her sparks

they left

her branded

stirred her

crazy like

the coffee

staining glass

between her

teeth so

she swung

axes at

their walls

until they

avalanched to

cinder once

swore their

love it

was contagious

now she

calls it


**- cabin fever**

**The Queer Community's Ode to the Oxford Comma**


We, too know how it feels

  to be best remembered

for the questioning of our importance.


To have our origin stories scribbled

across the white board

by those who seem the wisest,

only for dinner table conversations

to turn them into *well,*

*that's not how we were taught.*


We, too, falter at the pitch

  in our learner's voices

    when they call out:


*Teacher!*
*Why did you put that mark there?*


the same way they ask us:


*Hey, ▮▮▮▮ !*
*Are you a man or a woman?*

!,

*Why do you say spouse?*

*And not husband? Or wife?*

*Can we see your children,*

?

*Or, are they as invisible as you?*

We, too, have been erased from
the very worlds we helped create.
Are debated about as if
we are never in the room.

Expected to pause for another joke,
or ten, of our existence diminished to
attack helicopters,
sodomizing perverts,
and bathroom peeping toms,

when we are so much more
than the things we hold between us.

**Period Sex**

I once fell victim to a Venus

who, with the blood lust in her veins,

riddled me all the ways both moons

and mortals quenched her thirst in cycles


Said she'd never known such power

'til she'd gorged from crimson rivers,

lapped at the death of every Dawn before,

where arch to tongue met rosen ale,

a tongue her only weapon


and surely, that's how

her laughter learned to breed wounds,

a javelin to an unarmed chest,

when I declared I was an Eros,


why I swore I felt her heart

beat steady in my wrists

every time I slit them


why my lips puckered at the bitter

of copper in their garden

when she said:

*but darling,*

        *your blood is too*

                *sugar*

                    *and spice*

                        *nd cotton and vice*

                                *and darling,*

                                     *boys don't bleed*

                                        *like we do.*

**The Locusts and the Cottonwoods**

We will always have *that* drive to Lindo Lake.

Sitting bitch in Ryan's car,

all faith tossed between a wonky seatbelt,

two shy of a dozen change and tension sandwiches

we knew we'd never touch,

and a pocket full of names,

one common letter

we'd kept along the way.

And I will never understand

our curling-ironed blouse

or those strawberry wine pigtails,

and neither would the rest,

among too many other things

but still;

reeds we waded in the thickness,

unpacked our own picnic table epitaph,

counted every shade on Andrea's knee

twice, and then a dozen more

to fill what was lost.

but, if I had to guess,

I would say you knew

better than we all did

(among so many other things)

that this would be ~~their~~ our last goodbye,

buried underneath the eucalyptus and the oaks

and the tamaracks and the willows

and the pines and the locusts

and the cottonwoods,

a child without dinner,

and a hatchet been renamed,

only one common letter

we'd keep along the way.

**She**

She was a dancer.

And through her pointed feet
She told the narratives
her lips did not dare whisper out loud -

fairy tales and fantasies
torn from her spine at the seams
to replace with mystic tragedies.

Dragons who couldn't breathe fire
but still blistered her skin
with unloving hand prints
painted black and blue across
those pastel leotards She lived in.

Knights with shining armor
who sported breasts underneath.
That never saved her from her tower
but always came to sneak a peek
at her weakest hour; when the barre
slipping from beneath her fingertips
felt too far out of reach.

Melancholy in life,

yet a star on the stage.

She knew right where She belonged

from the moment She first

played in rosin like a sandbox.


And she could have stayed

forever in those studios

had She not begun to question

why boys never danced the way She did ‗

The heavens were not ready

to turn you to rainbows,

they only prayed for your storms to end.

- **heavens**

**He**

He was never a dancer.

But his feet still pointe by nature
each time He speaks of the stories
He was once too afraid to repeat -

dragons made obsolete
by two hands of his own
sacrificed for smothered flames
so his armor, one day,
could lie flat against his chest
while those old leotards
remained a fond, but distant memory.

Spotting stardom in life,
yet missing the home He once built
of heavy curtains and stadium seats.
For, now, he knows why
the boys never danced the way He did.
But has yet to figure out
just how to match the strides
of the other boys He envies

when all He's ever known remains

barre and rosin and a body

too small, turned out,

round in all the places it shouldn't be

and the same little-boy-blue ribbons

She once tied noose around her buns

before She became He.

**Hermit**

It is such a natural thing

that when one has

              o u t g r o w n    their shell

they shall,

          simply

                    seek a new one.

I cannot make bottles of my chest

or steal your rib to make me whole.

So, I must shape your bones

from building blocks

and finger paint your soul.


**- Baby Blue II**

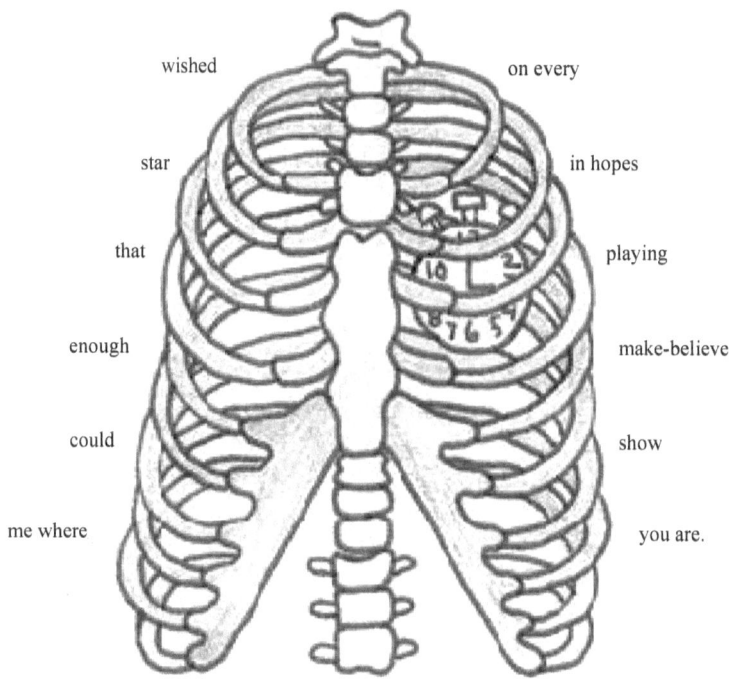

I've set my body clock to lullabies, wished on every star in hopes that playing make-believe enough could show me where you are.

- **Baby Blue III**

**Her Recycled Sock (Remains Unsure of What They are Building Today)**

sews its home inside her jeans

in an attempt ~~to confuse to world~~

~~to confuse herself~~

to ~~confuse~~ make some sense

out of her caverns and creases

with its crumpled up cotton,

thinking, surely

this is just another

one of their arts-and-crafts projects:

How-To-Build: A girl ~~the other~~ boys will want to settle down with.
How-To-Build: ~~A girl~~ boys ~~will choose~~ to pine over.

How-To-Build: ~~A girl~~ the other boys ~~will take~~ seriously.
How-To-Build: ~~A better girl for~~ boys.

How-To-Build: A perfect ~~girl for~~ boys.
How-To-Build: A normal ~~girl for~~ boys.

How-To-Build: A ~~girl into a~~ boy.

**Pulse**

In my third-grade gym class, they taught us how to check our pulse:

To mold our fingers into check marks,

check the box

between tendons on our wrists,

tenderly tough the skin

'til we feel the tip-taps

against our fingertips

and count the signs of life.

What should have been a rather insignificant day of elementary education

soon became the most fascinating investigation

for every wide-eyed, nine-year-old

Nancy Drew on the blacktop

when they realized that my heart

was determined to find a beat

faster than everyone else's.

My classmate's questions were jawbreakers that filled lips too full to swallow down.

They asked if my arteries

had learned to tap dance

from keeping tabs on my feet.

If my EKG could craft sound waves,

form beats for MTV deejays.

If my rib cage were the monkey bars,

would I be winning every race?

They asked if this meant I was going to die.

And if I'd have known then that being trans or being queer

was scripted in my stars,

I probably would have

blamed the stereotype.

You know, the one that says

 none of us will ever learn how to drive.

Perhaps my body knew the only chance I had to fly

down a highway, was to keep it all inside?

Or maybe. I should have blamed it on the anticipation.

Of a lifetime locked in closets; the way that "forever"

weighs heavy on your chest

when spent suffocating

between seasonal coats and systematic oppression.

How depression seems to stick to LGBT skin

Like it's embedded in our glitter,

on religious figures

who preached acceptance as a filthy habit

while hiding hate speech underneath their own.

If I'd have known.

I could have blamed it on a future

where another day

meant another headline, reading:

*another tranny faggot's life taken into the hands of time,*


Another "panic defense", picket fence, picket line

casting separation to the skies

labeled as the Lord's work.

Another conservative circle jerk

with queer blood painted

in the palms of Psalms

bookmarked from beating bigotry

between its pages. Like another calvinistic wet dream,

climaxing to the cries coming from

another courtyard candlelit vigil.


I could have blamed it on my Latino blood.

How its colors blend into our rainbows

Because if there's one thing

us queers and us Latinos

share between us


it's that we love a good up-beat.


Something quick,

something flavorful,

something we can dance to.

Because us queers and us Latinos,

We all love to fucking dance.

Those queer Latinos in Florida,

They just wanted to fucking dance

and now for an entire fucking community

the word "Pulse"

has an entirely different meaning.


I mean. Blamed it on the memories.

A moment of silence as serene

as crime scene caution tape.

The influx of notifications

that illuminated my face

on the ride home from

a local gay bar

I could never step foot in again

without counting all the exits.


Without playing hide-and-seek

with imaginary friends

behind barstools

and bathroom stalls

to plan escape with my real ones

should our gay bars be next

to transform into a gun range

without out consent.

Without the metamorphosis

of the words: *Please,*

*let me know when you're home safe*

from a request to a demand

because I can't dare fall asleep

after a night out

'til I know they're tucked in safe

without the nightmares seeping through

the cracks in their teeth.

Girl, I love that lipstick on you

but why do they

have to call it blood red?


My classmates asked if this meant I was going to die

and I should have told them:

*No.*

*Not then.*

*Not now.*

*Not ever.*

This entire community

was built behind bricks

meant to be thrown.

The Sun was meant to be felt on our faces

not leaving us

nameless and misgendered

underneath another shitty headline

where every time I scroll through,

I've got to check the story inside.


Mold my fingers into check marks,

check the box

between tendons on my wrists,

tenderly touch the skin

'til I feel the tip-taps

against my fingertips

and count the signs of life.

**Yellow : Tangerine : Bittersweet**

Yellow is my friend with a sunlit mile

who can light up a room

like it's Christmas -fucking- morning

any day of the year.

She is watchful.

She is slow;

center of the stoplight,

so ready to get fired up,

her queen bee jowl bowls wax

and live intentions,

then a district glowing red,

and she

is crime scene caution tape,

flashlights through car windows,

lemon liqueur sour on the breath of other girls

who only bother to recognize her yellow

once they've peeled her skin apart like tangerine.

**Cirque du Comparaison**

after Andrea Gibson


on your first day, / those who kept the grounds chest wife-beating / shared spit with feet turnt to mud / lent an eyeball / or four / to the softness of your creature / and low-voiced / ***there's no place, here / for someone like you / but, they all had to start somewhere / I 'spose.***

//

you were given one job / to scale inside the tent / day in / and day out / without stopping / you say / ***easy enough*** / out loud / in your head / until you say / ***fuck-shit*** / until you say / that you never realized / worms did not need can openers / until you / take that first step / up the vinyl and look down / to see worms / breeding from your mouth / until there are worms / slapping the concession stand-er / upside the head / and you find / he has pocketed them / for later.

//

soon / you will find / he will be the first / boy-who-likes-boys / to kiss you / you are twenty years young / spinning cotton candy / in his bedsheets / he becomes all too familiar / with the texture / of your sweet tooth / and you / having never known the taste / of a sugar rush before / from boys / who liked other boys / and didn't make a profit / off their limits / think / maybe / all things sweet / are made of fucking worms / except for him / and maybe you / if you are so lucky.

//

you think about the lion tamer / from Dorset / who is lulling a griffiness to sleep in the corner / how his roar / is so much louder / than yours / his roar / owns itself in ways / you have already deemed impossible / your roar / asks how he tames his inner beasts / and when his jaw snaps open / starving / there is nothing / but guitar strings / *there is nothing / I can teach you / from in here* / he spits / and you / spit-fire back / but not really / almost become a cannon-ball / but not just yet / your mew / sings while you are screaming / while you are bombing / from an eighth 'til the rooftop / *but I never learned / this goddamn melody / and I / just wanna be strong / like you* -

//

the jester / has you screaming / when your pride runs sore / has you beaming / while your thoughts / are all throat-shredded conversations / with your own reflection / wondering / if you'd / have carved yourself / a better backbone / had you never ceased / from splintering / your own toes / too / wondering why / they claim him / clown / when no strength / seems greater / than he who juggles / everything / you've ever feared / with everything / you ought to be / and calls it art / your house of mirrors / is begging you / *please / ask for the choreography / on how to strong-man / your useless bones / like that* / reigning / *perhaps you / could reunite your tarsals / with their shattered core / again.*

//

this time / you will try to reunite / the floorboards / again / try to break / your own fall / but not really / try to snap / your own neck / just right / but the snake charmer / will not let you / the snake charmer / grabs the pillbox / by its tail / from your gullet / and chucks it / into the away / from your bloodstream / he reminds you / what it's like / to be on fire / here / you are reminded / that it / too / was never / that you don't like boys / but that you only / like boys / you want to be / and you will try / you will try / you will try / you will try / to lick his wounds clean / and taste your own bloodbath / even when the snakes / just won't stop biting / won't stop fucking / hissing / wont stop / gumming / on your common sense / 'cause after all / if not for him / would you even / be alive / to try / you say / *that has to mean* / *has to count for somethin'* / *right?*

//

you say / **hush** / to your own anomaly / every day / you say / *oh* **I** *fuck* / *you* / while breaking / into the skin / of the ticket booth / like there is no double-feature / call it / the best admission ever spent / all seventy bucks / and seven seasons / of little sleep / to lock the door / throw away / your own larynx / your own face / for a while / let his disposition / sword-swallow you whole / even / when it knows / *you do not belong* / *in here* / call it / front row seat / to your most unrealistic ambition / call it never / enough pocket change / enough bleach / in this shitty place / in this wondrous place / in this god-damned / fuck-shit place / for a one-way ticket / in his direction / and damn / if he isn't / just a little flesh and own / and that tent / isn't just / scrap fabric / that you / can't stop / fucking / climbing / but damn / if there ever was / then you just might

//

and one day / so far from here / you just might realize / that it won't matter / how high you climb / because you will always / be looking up / that it won't matter / how many years / pass this / comparison circus by / because you / will never / not be there / because they / will never / not be there / the ringmasters / who wear whatever the fuck they want / and still / look like themselves / contortionists / who always shake your fist / with their jaw / and call you names / you've yet to untangle / the mimes / who taught you more / with their resilience / than with their hands / the tightrope heroes / who tell mom at the dinner table / that they are gay / that they are a man / that they are not / a part / of the freak show / and she tells them / to pass the peanuts / boys / with their stadium chests / and stilt-walk legacies / they didn't have to earn / the brothers / you always saved / your pennies for / but never / got to see / up close / or did you / the men / with their eyes / on a clothesline / living as a version of you / you've only seen / when you are sleeping / when you are dreaming

//

when you / were twenty years younger / grandstanding at about / three foot too / mouse to play / in the downpour / of your face / growing your own / elephant ears / to drown out / the applause / of bullets / watching for sliding glass / when your makers / low-voiced / *if you* / *want to be like them* / *so badly* / *why don't you* / *just run away* / *and join their circus* / and maybe / you did / in one way or another / maybe / you did / when you started scaling / this world of manhood / without any protection / with welcomed blisters / on your palms / with no flashing signs / to warn you / it would be / this goddamn hard / to find the exit / and now / every which way / you turn / there is an audience / waiting / wondering / when you / are going to be / more like them / and you / are still begging / out loud / in your head:

*don'tletgo / don'tletgo / don'tletgo / don'tletgo / don'tletgo / don'tletgo / don'tletgo / don'tletgo / don'tletgo / don'tletgo / don'tletgo / don'tletgo / don't letgo / don't letgo / don't letgo / don't letgo / don't letgo / don't letgo / don't letgo / don't letgo / don't letgo / don't letgo / don't letgo / don't letgo / don't let go / don't let go / don't let go / don't let go / don't let go / don't let go / don't let go / don't let go / don't let go / don't let go / don't let go / don't let go / don't let go / don't let go / don't let go / don't let go / don't let go / don't let go / don't let go / don't let go / don't let go / don't let go / don't let go / don't let go / don't / let go / don't / let go / don't / let go / don't / let go / don't/let go / don't/let go / don't/let go / don't/let go / don't/let go / don't/let go / don't/let go / don't/let go / don't/let go / don't/let go / don't / let go / don't / let go / don't / let go / don't / let / go / don't / let go / don't / let / go / don't / let go / don't / let / go / let / go / let / go / let / go / let / go / don't –*

losing you

was the greatest

love poem

ever written.

- **First Body**

**Password Security Questions for Transphobes on Twitter**

Option 1: What is your mother's maiden name?

And did its letters welt your fingertips

when you diminished another woman

down to her ability

to carry your budding burdens

exactly where you want them?

Option 2: What did you want to be when you grew up?

And how did it feel

having an answer other than

*dead before the puberty hit,*

or, *to survive long enough*

*to outlive your own hashtag trends and headlines?*

Option 3: What is your favorite color?

And why are you so afraid

of those who have blended

pink and blue

when purple is regality

and strength and dignity

and you are just

another keyboard warrior?

Truthfully, these

terms and conditions are simple.

You will need at least eight letters

to secure your argument,

and they cannot spell out

god,

church,

or only one percent of the population.

Final Question: Can you check the box to prove that you are even human?

That your hearts beat just like ours do?

**Anemoia**

*anemoia (n). nostalgia for a time you have never known*

Pluto has always been

the planet furthest from The Sun,

until he was not.

Before Pluto died,

and then came back to life,

again,

his orbit would play

double-dutch with Neptune's

every two hundred

and forty-eight years,

spend another twenty

thatmuchcloser to

the only child of Helios,

and then return.

Pluto, reborn

a poor, star-crossed romantic;

one too many times

to remember such phenomena;

too small, too juvenile

for the other planets

to find time to explain it,

knows only from

the icepick carving

sixth sense from his core,

that somehow, some way,

in some life lived before

or in a universe beyond this one

he and The Sun were -

something.

They were

something,

maybe,

Maybe, there was a time

Pluto could hold The Sun

between his palms and not burn.

Maybe they only held hands, like,

once, a long, long time ago,

but when they did,

the moon illuminating pale faces

through Pluto's basement window,

they agreed it was the best day

of their lives

without saying a word.

Maybe, they were 2am

in the pitch dark of a sleepover,

whispering their deepest, darkest secrets

after all the other cosmos went to sleep.

Maybe The Sun thought he wasn't

the dating type, until Pluto lead him

along the beach, let the tide kiss

their toes, and let The Sun kiss him

- everywhere.

Maybe they snuck out after twilight.

Found a 24-hour diner.

Stuck their straws into the milky way

and sipped until their brains took off running.

Maybe, they waited each night

for the new artists to paint-splatter

stars into the sky

and called it time to creep home

before The Sandman found out.

Maybe The Sun tasted

like strawberry Lip Smackers,

and would always leave a pink lipped trail

around his end of the paper cup telephone.


Maybe The Sun had awful bedhead

and Pluto had bad morning breath

and they've worn glitter on their skin

and flutters in their hearts

and nervous smiles, all at once.


Maybe, Pluto had a sweet spot

at the pulse point on his neck,

and The Sun was the only

one in the know.


Maybe The Sun

started to get belly aches

every time they were apart.


Maybe they held their hands in wet cement

outside of The Sun's high school theatre,

where he rehearsed how to cry over Venus

so nobody would know he was gay.

Maybe they were prom dates.

Maybe Pluto held The Sun's hair back
while he got sick in the parking lot,
and they never spoke of it again.

Maybe, they just stared at each other
for a little too long in homeroom
but never said a word.
Went their separate ways at lunch
but never heard the end of it
at slumber parties.

Maybe, they fell asleep every night.
The Sun's head on Pluto's chest.
Maybe he melted all his ice caps.
Maybe he gathered all his rocks
and chucked them into the atmosphere.

Maybe they always took turns
being the little spoon.

Maybe, they had two sets of parents.
Two days of Christmas present opening.
Two fridges waiting to be raided.
Two ways to hide underneath covers

when they did not want to be found.

Maybe, The Sun's love language
was gifts, and Pluto's quality time.
So, Pluto always brought iced coffee
and fast food with a toy inside
when The Sun would take them
the long way 'round the galaxy.

Maybe they were a letterman
during a meteor shower.
Shouldering The Sun's rays
to keep him safe and warm until
they waded through backseat,
past crap littered floor
and laughed nervously, while Pluto fumbled
with fingers on buttons
and lips in uncharted places.

Maybe, The Sun snuck in
through Pluto's bedroom window
and taught him how
to roll a joint.

Maybe, The Sun came home
to Pluto on his darkest days,

uninvited and unannounced,

washed his tangled depression

in the sink, slipped him into something

a little less concerning - kicking and screaming

if he had to - and just stayed with him

until Pluto felt almost normal again.


Maybe they were kids again,

a-and they played with Hot Wheels

and little, yellow dogs

and made their Barbies kiss

until they were not afraid to anymore.


Maybe, they rode down every other

cliche' avenue of the 20-something-poet

trying to build an imaginary home in

both places they have never been

and places they shouldn't have.


Maybe, The Sun held on to Pluto

in the silence, rocked him back

and forth and back and forth

and back and forth and


Maybe, they didn't belong

to the sky at all-maybe, they were e-mails

or, or voicemails,

or instant fucking messages.


Hell, maybe they were plants.

Ryegrasses and shade trees

pulling baby teeth out

from each other's roots

when the playground wasn't looking.


Or-or they were dogs,

sniffing each other's necks

every Saturday at the dog park,

trying desperately to retain the scent

so they could find their way back home.


Or maybe they were humans,


watching with fingers

nineteen years young latched

around a kaleidescope of matter,


a stethoscope of nothing,

and everything all at once


a telescope, screaming

*"I know you! I know you-*

*are somewhere. I know you*

*are somewhere and you are*

*waiting for me too. And I know you*

*are too good to be*

*come true from simply wishing*

*on a star,*

*so I found*

*the brightest one in the sky*

*and I wait for you*

*every sunrise."*

**04/09/2019**

I do not know the hands who built us.

But, I do believe they should be fired.

Tried on the grounds of playing

a modern day Frankenstein.

That is to say,

who else could they have been

if not a recreational sadist

who once hid us in their tool shed

for unsafe keeping?

Maniacal and laughing

as they sifted through

the box of our world's

formerly rejected parts?

The ones marked *caution.*

*Ineffective.*

*Do not disturb.*

*Do not attempt to reassemble*

*as it will put us at risk.*

For, could that not explain

how so many of us

recall ourselves so patchwork strung?

His hands on her body?

Her body with his scowl?

His scowl on their hips?

Their heart blossomed

amongst vessels once deemed

not worth the salvage?

For, could that not explain

how we have had to mend ourselves

as if we've all been rusted for renew?

Repaying debts we did not obtain?

Repenting for a ruse we did not act upon?

**Euphemism for Pissing**

You leave to take a bathroom break,

and you are still perfecting

how to piss standing up,

because you only started learning

how to piss standing up a week ago,

and you are still intimidated

by alligator mouth

gaping inside porcelain swamp,

reminding you that you are twenty-six,

and in the middle of a poetry workshop

where you can still hear the

clatter of a poem about suicide

from the next room over,

and that most boys do not learn

how to piss standing up

at twenty-six, as grown men,

or staring into the same porcelain

they once used to flush

their own suicidal ideation,

or with a rubber funnel clamped

between trembling thumb and four fingers

to makeshift an anatomy they do not have

and you cannot shake the tension

of the invisible clock ticking to your death,

and the alligator is asking

if this will be the time - the only time,

thus far, that you will return

undampened and undefeated,

and what impression it may leave

if you are gone for too long,

returning, dripping an elegy

onto your papers and the desk chair;

so, you unlearn how to piss standing up

for just one more day

- OR -

You leave to take a bathroom break,

and you are still perfecting

how to piss standing up,

because you only started learning

how to piss standing up a week ago,

and you are still intimidated

by alligator mouth

gaping inside porcelain swamp,

reminding you that you are twenty-six,

and in the middle of a poetry workshop

where you can still hear the

clatter of a poem about suicide

from the next room over,

and that most boys do not learn

how to piss standing up

at twenty-six, as grown men,

or staring into the same porcelain

they once used to flush

their own suicidal ideation,

or with a rubber funnel clamped

between trembling thumb and four fingers

to makeshift an anatomy they do not have,

but you do it without thinking,

and it is as unmemorable,

as uneventful

as taking a piss could be imagined

- OR -

You leave to take a bathroom break,

and you are still perfecting

how to piss standing up,

not because you only started learning

how to piss standing up a week ago,

but because you are

just clumsy and anxious

and a little bit awkward

in most situations

and you are still intimidated

by alligator mouth

gaping inside porcelain swamp,

reminding you that you are twenty-six,

and in the middle of a poetry workshop

where you can still hear the

clatter of a poem about suicide

from the next room over,

and you wonder if any of them know

that you left to piss standing up,

staring into the same porcelain

you once used to flush

your own suicidal ideation,

but, thankfully,

you learned how to piss standing up

roughly twenty-three years ago and

you were born with the right anatomy

to piss standing up without thinking

and it is as unmemorable,

as uneventful

as taking a piss could be imagined.


So, you just piss,

and do not even think to write an elegy about it.

**Inferno**

Devils never dwell

when holy tongues

craft torches of their tails,

for they have seared

the paths to prove

thou shalt move on

one step ahead.

**Asexual Musings**

Home alone was an awful name for a movie,

and is an even worse way to begin a poem,

but is the best time to cry while wearing a strap-on.

I should have known

when my first girlfriend

laughed at my attempts to be sexy.

True story:

I hit my head while losing my virginity.

Perhaps, that just knocked

the sex appeal right out of me.

I have, on more than one occasion,

faked an interest in browsing

butt plugs or nipple clamps

at the local sex shop,

before "settling" on the wand vibrator

I knew I came in to buy

to make it seem like I was

"cool" and "sexually active"

and not just buying it for chronic back pain.

I was so lonely last Christmas

that I responded to some stranger on the Internet

who wanted to sext me, quickly realized

I would rather consume my own fingers

than sext strangers on the Internet,

but kept the conversation going until they had finished

because I still feared what could happen

if I proved to be another disappointment.


This may seem like an isolated incident,

but spare a few details

this story could be told

for almost any sexual encounter I've had.


Repulsive.

Disaster.

Repulsive.

Disaster.

Repulsive. Disaster.

Repulsive. Disaster.

Repulsive disaster.


I WANT to want to have sex;

but I just don't want to WANT to want have sex;

enough to actually want to have sex.

My favorite sex story

is the one where me and at least

ten of my not-closest friends

were dogpiled in an iHop at 1:37 in the morning,

syrup dripping down our sweaty bodies,

stuffing our face holes with potato hash,

unprotected and arguing over

whether it was possible

to be your own grandparent.


At some point,

I will probably still suck a dick

just to say that I have;

and that it was not yours this time.


I will never forget you,

tiny human with the massive dildo collection.

And that, is an unfortunate reality.


I wish the reality of the phrase "birthday suits"

lived up to the expectation.

Mine would be fitted and pinstriped

with a cone-style hat to match

and not this dusty, old mantle

with far too many fingerprints upon it.

I have probably faked an orgasm more times

than I have given myself a real one.

The rest of my body is so fucked up

that I would not be in disbelief to find

the erogenous zones were never installed,

or were misplaced somewhere

they will never be found

like between my nasty toes

or underneath an eye socket.

Is this sexual attraction,

or do I just enjoy the warmth?

I often wonder whether I will end up

with someone else asexual,

or they will have to learn to settle for me.

I am not sure I have a preference.

I am not sure either are without guilt.

Or, maybe, perhaps,

there is some alternate universe

where my life partner and I

can have a ~~normal~~ sex life

without the gut wrenching panic

before taking our pet pigs out for a fly.

What would I be if I had never met you?


On the list of things I have done for attention,

all the times I have Pinocchio-ed

my way through sex

just to be another's puppet

has to be the most pathetic.


The phrase "ace in the hole"

sounds awfully ironic

if you switch up the context.


An ace who was formerly branded

as their high school slut

sounds awfully ironic,

even with the proper context.


Why, yes,

there are eggplants on my underwear,

thank you for noticing.

I have the same cursed sense of humor

as cis men who hang nut sacks from their trucks.


When I say that I would have fucked them,

what I really mean is that

it may have been worth disassociating for

those three to ten minutes

(on average,

according to Google)

to earn that spot in their bed

with their head on my chest

while they drifted off to sleep afterwards.


Shoutout to the hookup

who asked if she could make me a sandwich after.

That was one

damn good


sandwich.


Perhaps, *this* wouldn't be

so hard

if my body could be.


I still cannot confidently tell you

what a penis actually looks like.


I do not miss the sex

but I do miss being touched

by so many hands who claimed to love me.

Do I spend the extra $100

for a packer that can get hard

or do I just assume I will die alone

and relieved?


Hey Siri,

am I still asexual if I have a thing for hickies

and necks and soft, dark hair and the smell

of a person who smells like home and holding

hands all the fucking time and giggling over

the accidental titty graze when going in for

a hug and knobby knees and the way butts

in skinny jeans fit onto my lap

while we're kissing for hours and hours

and girls who get excited when they find

pockets in their dresses and boys

who wear makeup and freckles and bruises?


In the Sims, there are fireworks

every time someone gets laid.

In my world, there are fireworks

when I see someone attractive in the drive-thru

and not a minute longer.

What does that say about us?


Do not worry, ladies of Tinder,

I am not trying to fuck you.

I am, however, already planning our wedding,

and the names of our three adopted children,

one of which actually being an Australian Shepherd.

Maybe,

the thought of Jesus or Santa

always watching me just never left my head

and maybe, I am just not a voyeur.

If you had to make me ~~untouchable~~ ace,

why did you also have to make

physical touch one of my love languages?

Can't  we   just

kiss   a    little

longer *please* ?


One time, a cryptid suggested we watch porn together

and one time, another time,

I switched out the audio

for one of those shitty, coming of age movies

so, it was just people crying out

 "Yes! More! Just like that!"

while driving cross country with their friends

and growing whipped cream mustaches in diners

and screaming at rooftops in the middle of the big city

and hugging each other really, really tight.

And I hope one day

we can both forgive my body

for chasing other dreams

that chased your home away.

**- Baby Blue IV**

**Blink**

Imagine

what it must look like

to be free:

the hot air balloon

on their first trip to infinity,

or neverland,

or your optometrist's office,

or wherever took them

furthest away from *there* -

the land that forced

their lids zipped tight;

cried wolf the nights they slept

with one eye open

    *just in case*;

Yet still,

taught them not to blink.

That in the blink of an eye,

one small town,

small minded,

mind over manners,

small world,

world view

could				shift

		change

set sail somewhere

uncharted and unfamiliar

and made them wonder.

*what would be so wrong about that,*

*anyways?*

**Acknowledgments**

First and foremost, Blink would not be the same without Mallory's incredible artistry bringing my words to life. An endless thank you to her for being all in from day one and putting up with all of the insanely long emails, medical interferences, and my complete inability to stick to deadlines.

I am eternally grateful for the spaces and the people within them that kept my poetry alive through the shit-storm that was the year 2020: Desiree Dallagiacomo's *Undercurrent*, Neil Hilborne's *Writing Circle*, Nicole Tracii's *Chapbook Chatter*, The Venue on 35th, Zeider's American Dream Theater, and - of course, *Rainbow Writers*.

Special thanks to Nicole, Ellora, Lary, Myles, Ceryn, Rameen, and Brook "Tuesday" for the endless hours of editing help and pep talks, to Chrissy for introducing me to the art of slam poetry and its existence in virtual space, and to Beth for introducing me to Ella - without whose guidance I never would have seen such progress so quickly.

To my chosen family: Mackenzie, Wren, Ryan, Tyler, Aunt "Taytee", Riley, Joshua, Michael, Zachary, Leigh, and all others who supported and/or inspired me in this endeavor. This lost boy is so lucky to have found a home in you all in one way or another.

**About the Author**

Sawyer ( he/they) is a writer, teacher, and future adolescent counselor from San Diego, CA, now residing in Virginia Beach, VA. His body of work thus far is greatly inspired by his experiences as a queer, trans individual and a survivor of stage four endometriosis. In 2020, alongside working on *Blink*, they also founded the web-based writing workshop *Rainbow Writers* as a cost-free creative space for queer, trans, and questioning poets. You can keep up with all of Sawyer's future writing endeavors on Instagram at @sbc.poetry.

**About the Illustrator**

Mallory (she/her) was born and raised in Virginia Beach, VA. Although this was her first experience with illustration, she has been blessing the 757 with her incredible artistry for several years. Mallory's personal artwork, referred to as a "visual representation of her brain", often focuses on canvas paintings and can be found on Instagram at @_malloryblue.

www.ingramcontent.com/pod-product-compliance
Lightning Source LLC
Chambersburg PA
CBHW030915080526
44589CB00010B/317